A BOOT UP

NEWCASTLE
& GATESHEAD

Anthony Toole

First published in Great Britain in 2013

British Library Cataloguing-in-Publication Data
A CIP record for this title is available from the British Library

ISBN 978 0 85710 078 8

PiXZ Books
Halsgrove House, Ryelands Business Park,
Bagley Road, Wellington, Somerset TA21 9PZ
Tel: 01823 653777
Fax: 01823 216796
email: sales@halsgrove.com

An imprint of Halstar Ltd, part of the Halsgrove group of companies
Information on all Halsgrove titles is available at: www.halsgrove.com

Printed and bound in China by Toppan Leefung

Contents

How to use this book

The Area

In AD 120, around the time of the construction of Hadrian's Wall, the Romans built a bridge over the River Tyne between what are now Newcastle and Gateshead, and thirty years later, a fort to defend it. Newcastle's name derives not from this fort, but from the castle built there by the Normans in AD 1080.

Coal was mined in the north-east as early as the 2nd century AD, though the activity was sporadic and small scale. By the 13th century, however, trade in the fuel had become brisk along the coast, and there were mines in the area during the late Tudor period. Indeed, use of the colloquialism, 'carrying coals to Newcastle', to express the ultimate in futility, dates from the 1530s.

Coal was easily extracted in the area, as it lay near the surface, and could be brought to the ports on the Tyne by a network of railways. Initially, coal wagons were drawn by horses, though by the early 19th century, these were being replaced by the steam locomotives that were developed in the region for that purpose by pioneers such as George and Robert Stephenson and Timothy Hackworth. Unlike elsewhere in Britain, there were no canals in the north-east.

Though there remains much coal to be found here, it has been superseded by cheaper imports and cleaner hydrocarbon fuels and the last deep mine closed in 2005. The decline of mining was accompanied by those of other heavy industries, such as armaments manufacturing at Elswick and ship-building at Wallsend, so that very little of what sustained the Industrial Revolution remains.

Yet the relics of the once-powerful industries cannot easily be erased. With assistance from the Newcastle and Gateshead Councils, and the Northumberland and Durham Wildlife Trusts, they have been transformed into parks and Nature reserves. Barren pit heaps have become flower-covered grasslands. Subsidence hollows are now water filled, their reed-bed fringes providing shelter for wildfowl. The cut-

1 Big Waters

A 3¼-mile walk around a surprising haven of peace and wildlife that lies beneath the flight path of Newcastle Airport.

Until quite recently, a cluster of collieries dotted the fields around a patch of countryside some five miles to the north of Newcastle upon Tyne city centre. Between 1960 and 1985, these mines closed down, leaving a network of underground tunnels, which collapsed to form a series of subsidence ponds that were quickly taken over by Nature, aided by sensitive landscaping. The largest of these is Big Waters, a Site of Special Scientific Interest and a Northumberland Wildlife Trust nature reserve. Many birds breed in the surrounding woods and extensive reedbeds, their number swelled by visiting migrants in winter.

Level: 🥾
Length: 3¼ miles
Terrain: Surfaced road, rubble tracks and grassy footpaths.
Park & start: Car park ½ kilometre north of the Wideopen-Dinnington road, sign-posted just after the houses of Brunswick Village.
Start ref.: NZ 229732
Public transport: The 45 bus from Newcastle passes through Gosforth, Wideopen, Brunswick and Dinnington.
Websites: www.nwt.org.uk

Big Waters from the south shore.

Go through the gateway at the northern end of the car park, and follow the footpath to the left, which leads to the lake shore. Continue (NE then E) along the shore, past the outflow, stepping stones and a bridge. Carry on along the river bank for 300 metres, through grassland scattered with hazel, alder, hawthorn, blackthorn and dog rose, to reach a second footbridge, where the burn runs beneath the A1 road. The metal structure that runs through the culvert is an otter bridge.

Cross the footbridge and return by the north bank of

The otter bridge.

the burn to the end of the lake. Follow the track that curves round toward the north, past two small patches of woodland, to join a farm road.

Turn left (W). After 200 metres, where the road turns into North-east Mason Farm, carry on along the cycle track, past a private track and a series of fields.

After 1100 metres, the track turns left (S) and back right

Resident birds on Big Waters pond include gulls, mallards, herons, coots, moorhens, cormorants and great crested grebes. Among winter visitors are whooper swans and pink-footed geese.

Stepping stones across the outflow.

Boardwalk in the nature reserve.

(WSW) after another 100 metres. A further 250 metres brings you to a junction. Turn left (S) and continue for 250 metres to a bridge over a stream.

5 Cross the bridge, and at the next bend, 50 metres farther, go through the kissing gate (E) into a

field. Follow the boardwalk and the edges of this field and the next, to a junction with the previously encountered private track. Continue on this, which is no longer private, for 50 metres, then go through the next gate. After 150 metres, reach the corner of the wood that lies to the

Bird feeding station.

The building of the otter bridge, to prevent deaths of otter cubs crossing the main road, featured in a 2006 Channel 4 television documentary, Wild Thing I Love You, presented by comedian Bill Bailey. Stoats as well as otters now use the bridge.

south-west of Big Waters lake. Another 350 metres brings you to the gateway into the Nature Reserve.

6 It is worth making a detour into the reserve. Keys to the

Common visitors to the feeding station are blue tits, long-tailed tits, siskins, goldfinches, chaffinches, greenfinches, pheasants and great spotted woodpeckers.

Rabbit, moorhen and pheasant at the feeding station.

Goldfinch at the feeding station.

Following reclamation work, between 1969 and 1974, Newcastle University carried out a study at Big Waters into the development of grasslands and woodlands on former industrial sites.

two bird hides are held only by members of the Northumberland Wildlife Trust, but a dipping pond and bird feeding station are readily accessible from the boardwalk of re-cycled plastic that runs along the southern reedbeds.

From the entrance gate to the reserve, carry on to the next patch of woodland, and turn left (N) to return to the start.

Cormorants on an artificial island.

2 **Havannah Nature Reserve**

An easy, though sometimes muddy 2-mile walk through a mosaic of wildlife habitats, adjacent to Newcastle Airport.

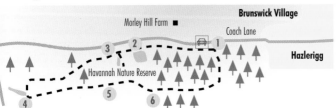

Morley Hill Farm ■

Brunswick Village

Coach Lane

Hazlerigg

Havannah Nature Reserve

Level:
Length: 2 miles
Terrain: Rough track and grassy footpaths.
Park & start: 250 metres beyond the west end of Hazlerigg Village, a signpost pointing to Three Hills indicates a small car park.
Start ref.: NZ 226718
Public transport: No. 44 bus from Newcastle.
Websites: www.newcastle.gov.uk

Lying alongside the road that runs from Hazlerigg to Newcastle Airport, yet strangely unaffected by the noise of the latter, is the exotic-sounding Havannah Nature Reserve. Comprising more than 40 hectares of woodland, marsh, heath, hay meadow and pond, this wildlife haven occupies the site of the former Havannah Colliery, which closed down in 1977, after 27 years' production, to prevent subsidence of the runways when the airport was extended. Indeed, the evidence for its industrial past is seen in the now water-filled subsidence hollows and the embankments and bridleway that mark the route of the old rail track.

Peacock butterfly.

Approaching the east pond.

1 Follow the bridleway (W) that leads from the entrance to the car park through mixed woodland comprising sycamore, ash, oak, hazel and birch. Alternatively, take the sometimes muddy footpath that converges with the bridleway. After 350 metres, step over the low barrier at the edge of the wood onto open scrubland. 100 metres farther is the first, and largest, of the ponds, fringed with patches of soft rush. Mute swans have nested here for a number of years, raising several broods of cygnets. A heron often stalks the shallow margins.

Swans on the east pond.

2 Continue along the bridleway, on the north side of which lies a series of shallow pools, overhung by

The shallow pools on the north side of the bridleway, near the main pond, often dry up in warm weather, but in springtime, become breeding grounds for frogs, as well as common and great crested newts.

Heathland and the east pond.

West pond.

dense gorse and hawthorn thickets. Just west of the main pond, a wooden boardwalk offers a short detour to a hidden region of hawthorn scrub and a smaller pond, fringed by tall reed mace, and populated by dragonflies.

3 The track leads on to a fork. Take the left fork, which snakes past the site of the Havannah Drift Mine, to a third pond, surrounded by birch, reeds and reed mace. Spring flowers growing on the damp surrounds include orchids, ragged

The Havannah drift mine, at its peak, employed 870 people. Its alternative name, Three Hills, refers to the three slag heaps that once occupied the site.

robin, water mint and yellow flag iris. The road from Dinnington to Newcastle lies a short distance farther, and beyond that, the boundary fence of Newcastle Airport.

4 Just after passing a wooden bench, where the bridleway makes a right angled turn, cross the stile to the left and follow the footpath (E) across a succession of hay

Hazlerigg and Brunswick villages were once separated by a railway line. They are now linked by a footpath that can be walked in under five minutes. The 2-mile road trip, through Wideopen, takes much longer.

Entrance to the forest.

meadows, which in summer are knee-deep in buttercups, purple and spotted orchids, ox-eye daisies, eyebright and the parasitic yellow rattle. These attract peacock, red admiral and skipper butterflies. Rabbits are abundant in the meadows. Lapwing and curlews are often seen in the adjacent cultivated fields.

5 At the eastern end of the third meadow, go through a kissing gate onto stone slabs, which lead across often swampy ground onto the heathland to the south of the

Coach Lane splits Hazlerigg village into two. The northern section belongs to North Tyneside, while the southern lies in Newcastle.

large pond. This area is colonised by birch, hawthorn, gorse and extensive carpets of heather.

6 Enter the wood via a stile at the south-east corner of the heath. Follow the boardwalk for 100

metres, then the gently rising path, which after 50 metres, crosses a second path. After a short distance, this descends to a junction with a broader track at a footbridge crossing over a deep ditch. Turn left (N) and follow the track for 200 metres to the car park.

Highland cows in hay meadow.

3 **Weetslade Hill**

A varied 3-mile walk up what is probably the highest hill in North Tyneside, and through one of the newest urban nature reserves in the area.

Weetslade Hill is a mining spoil heap, yet over the past few years, what was a stark, grey blot blocking the horizon north of Gosforth Park, has been transformed into an attractive, and still evolving wildlife refuge, managed by the Northumberland Wildlife Trust. The hill rises above former industrial land between Wideopen and Dudley, just to the west of Weetslade Farm. It is sandwiched between an old waggonway to the south and wetlands to the north. In summer, the southern slopes are a vivid blaze of gorse and broom, which provide shelter for the nests of many small birds and a hunting ground for kestrels.

Level: 🥾

Length: 3 miles

Terrain: Surfaced road, rubble and grassy footpaths.

Park & start: Car park near Weetslade Farm, on B1319, reached from roundabout linking A189 and A1056, just north of Gosforth Park.

Start ref.: NZ 260723

Public transport: None to the start. Frequent buses from Newcastle Haymarket to Wideopen pass points 4/5 of walk.

Websites: www.nwt.org.uk

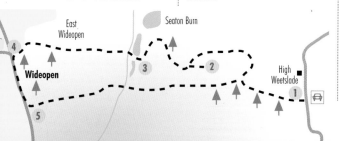

Teasel flower and burnet moths.

Weetslade Farm.

① Follow the surfaced footpath west out of the car park into Weetslade Country Park, and on for 300 metres to the foot of the hill. Turn right onto the gentle incline, which spirals around the north side of the hill before turning back to the summit, which is crowned by a sculpture representing the drill bits that were used in the local mines. From its height of 95 metres, the hill affords extensive views across the northern suburbs of Newcastle and on as far as County Durham. To the east lies the coast, while to the north-west and west are the Cheviot Hills, the Simonsides and the North Pennines.

② Re-trace the route (W) for 100 metres, then descend the rubble track that curves to the right,

Summit of Weetslade Hill.

Wetland to the north of the hill.

heading for the pond and wetlands that lie to the north of the hill. Near the base of the hill, the path curves back left, past a smaller pond, to a notice board and a gateway at the western limit of the hill.

③ Pass through the gateway (W), along a grassy track and across a footbridge over a small stream. Continue across a field and through a narrow strip of conifer woodland to East Wideopen Farm. Carry on in the same direction for 300 metres to join the road in Wideopen.

Weetslade Colliery stood 250 metres south-west of the start of the walk. It opened in 1903 and closed in 1966. Its main shaft was 350 metres (1140 feet) deep, and its workings linked with those at Burradon Colliery, a mile to the east.

Pond to the north of the hill.

The reedbeds and pools to the north-west of the hill provide the calm water environment in which Daubenton's bats can forage for insects such as midges and mayflies.

4 Turn left (ESE), past a children's playing field and follow the pavement for 300 metres to an opening onto the Havannah Mineral Line, just after passing the entrance to a housing estate. This is where a level crossing carried railway wagons from the Havannah Drift Colliery between 1950 and the closure of the mine in 1977.

5 Turn left (ENE) and follow the track. This leads through the housing estate and the tree-lined continuation of the waggonway. After 550 metres, a second track runs in from the left. Keep right, over a small burn and a bridge to re-enter Weetslade Country Park. Continue for 500 metres along the base of Weetslade Hill, and a further 500 metres beyond, back to the car park.

Signpost at the start of the Mineral Line.

A total of 14 miners lost their lives in accidents at Weetslade, five of them in a single explosion on 1 October 1951. Five more died from silicosis and pneumoconiosis.

View west from the lower slope of the hill.

Kidney vetch.

Bird's-foot-trefoil.

*Gorse and hawthorn blossoms,
on the southern slope of Weetslade Hill.*

4 Swallow Pond & Rising Sun Hill

A quiet and varied 3¼-mile walk around a remarkable haven for wildlife that is completely surrounded by urban sprawl.

Hiding behind a large supermarket, Wallsend Swallow Pond was formed by the collapse of the mineshafts of the Rising Sun Colliery, once the largest deep mine in Europe. It is home to coot, moorhen, mallard, tufted duck and mute swan, which nest in the surrounding reed beds. In winter, bird numbers are augmented by teal, pochard and redshank that roost on the artificial islands created from the rubble of demolition sites. Mammals found here include foxes, voles, hedgehogs, water shrews, roe deer and even a solitary red deer stag. Rising Sun Hill, a grassland habitat with patches of scrub and woodland, was created from the refuse of the mine. Landscaping, during the 1970s, reduced its height by a third.

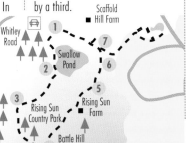

Level: 🥾 🥾
Length: 3¼ miles
Terrain: Grassy footpaths and cycle tracks.
Park & start: Car park beside Rising Sun Country Park, behind Benton ASDA supermarket on the A191, north of Wallsend.
Start ref.: NZ 302696
Public transport: Bus - No. 355, Newcastle-Whitley Bay, stops by ASDA supermarket.
Metro - Walk east from Palmersville station, on the Newcastle-Coast line, then turn right at roundabout to Country Park entrance.
Websites: www.northtyneside.gov.uk/ environment/risingsun

1 Turn right (WNW) from the car park and walk for 100 metres to a stile. Cross this onto a footpath between pastures (SSW), which leads, in 100 metres, into mixed woodland of conifer, birch and alder. After passing a dipping pond, follow the track to the left, alongside a fence. A wooden boardwalk leads past an area of damp grassland, which in spring and summer contains cowslips, ragged robin, bird's foot trefoil and marsh orchids, and attracts peacock, orange tip and painted lady butterflies. The boardwalk continues to a concrete hide, which gives a view over the pond and its bird populations. Continue on the footpath to join the Killingworth Waggonway.

Entrance to woodland.

Killingworth Waggonway opened in 1763 to transport coal to the River Tyne. George and Robert Stephenson, who lived at nearby Forest Hall, used the tracks to test their 'Rocket' locomotive, before entering it, successfully, in the Rainhill Trials of 1829.

Swallow Pond.

Opposite: *Artificial island, Swallow Pond.*

Killingworth Waggonway.

Swallow Pond & Rising Sun Hill

The Rising Sun Colliery had a shaft 1400 feet deep and 60 miles of underground tunnels, which extended as far as the River Tyne. At its peak, it employed 1800 miners. It closed in 1969.

2 Turn left (SE) and follow the waggonway for 70 metres to a junction. (A second bird hide is situated a further 70 metres along the waggonway.) Turn right (SSW) and follow the track for 300 metres to join the next waggonway, at the base of Rising Sun Hill. Go through the gateway and up the track for 250 metres to the top of the hill, from which there are extensive views over the surrounding urban areas of Wallsend and Newcastle.

3 Continue beyond the top for 50 metres, then turn left (SSE) onto a footpath that descends through and to the right of a narrow strip of woodland, and curves round to the left. Various tracks lead down across the grassland to join a road,

Bird hide, Killingworth Waggonway.

over which the remains of a railway track can be seen.

4 Turn left (N) and follow the road, which in 350 metres,

Urban view from Rising Sun Hill.

swings to the north-east, past the Rising Sun Organic Farm, which welcomes visitors. A further 200 metres brings you back onto the Killingworth Waggonway.

Rising Sun Organic Farm.

Turn right, then almost immediately left, and either follow the broad bridleway, or after a short distance, detour through Hadrian Woodland for 250 metres to the next junction.

6 Turn right, then after 150 metres, left over a wooden footbridge. A rough, and sometimes muddy track leads between a field and the housing estate to a wooden marker pole. Turn right over a second wooden bridge and across grassland and around a small scrub-covered hill

The car park to the east of the supermarket occupies the former site of miners' houses, known as Wapping Square. In 1929, these were visited by the then Prince of Wales.

to Hadrian Pond, the remnant of an ancient bog, which contains a rich array of fen vegetation and several rare species of beetle. After exploring this, return to point 6.

7 Turn right (WNW) and return,

in 400 metres, to the Country Park Visitor Centre and car park. On the way, it is possible to make a brief detour through an opening in the hedgerow on the right to see the water birds on Dukes Pond.

Hadrian Pond.

The Country Park Visitor Centre occupies the site of Scaffold Hill isolation hospital, which was in use between 1914 and 1986, treating infectious diseases such as diphtheria, tuberculosis and scarlet fever.

Rising Sun Country Park Visitor Centre.

5 NEWCASTLE & GATESHEAD QUAYSIDES

A continuously interesting 2¼-mile urban walk that gives architectural glimpses of the past, present and future of Newcastle and Gateshead.

Throughout the Industrial Revolution, Tyneside was the powerhouse that created much of Britain's wealth. As industry declined, so did the industrial centres. But the region that gave us the Stephensons, Joseph Swan, William Armstrong and others could not long remain dormant. From John Dobson's magnificent Central Railway Station, it is a short distance to the bridges of the Tyne, which range from the 18th century Swing Bridge to the 21st century Millennium Bridge. World class science is represented by the Centre for Life, while the Sage and Baltic provide the equivalents in the arts. Though this walk is short, one can spend the day visiting the several venues en route.

Level: 🚶
Length: 2¼ miles
Terrain: City pavements.
Park & start: Newcastle Central Railway Station.
Start ref.: NZ 246639
Public transport: Central Station is served by bus and Metro.
Websites: www.life.org.uk
www.balticmill.com
www.thesagegateshead.org

Centre for Life.

① Turn left (WSW) out of the main station entrance and walk for 300 metres to Times Square, which is surrounded by the Centre for Life. On the opposite side of the road, you will pass the Roman Catholic St Mary's Cathedral, on the steps of which is a bronze statue of the late Cardinal Basil Hume, who was a native of Newcastle. Cross Times Square onto Waterloo Street, turn left (SSE) and continue to the traffic lights.

Statue of Cardinal Basil Hume.

Newcastle Central Station.

② Turn left again (ENE) and go along Forth Street to a pedestrian crossing beneath the railway bridge. Cross the road and carry on for another 30 metres, before turning right (SE) and descending Forth Banks. The road curves to the left,

During spring, kittiwakes can be seen nesting on ledges on the Tyne Bridge and the Guildhall, eight miles from the coast. These are thought to be the farthest inland nesting kittiwakes in the world.

Tyne and Millennium bridges, Baltic and Sage.

The Tyne Bridge and the Sydney Harbour Bridge were built by Dorman Long of Middlesbrough to a similar design. The Sydney bridge was begun in 1923 and opened in 1932. The Tyne Bridge was commenced in 1925 and completed by 1928.

The Swing Bridge, opened in 1876, is able to rotate 360 degrees, using the original machinery, designed by Lord William Armstrong. Along with the High Level Bridge and the Central Station, it appears in the Newcastle-based 1971 film, 'Get Carter.'

Swing Bridge and High Level Bridge from Tyne Bridge.

beneath the Queen Elizabeth II (railway) Bridge. Directly under the bridge, turn right, through a car park to join a footpath and cycleway that runs along the quayside.

3 Turn left (NE) and walk along the quayside for 450 metres, beneath the High Level Bridge, to reach the Swing Bridge. Go through the arch on the left and up the steps beyond and to the left, then turn left again onto the Newcastle end of the Swing Bridge. Cross the bridge to Gateshead.

4 Follow the pavement that curves to the left, uphill and under the Tyne Bridge. Continue for 450 metres, past the Sage Concert

Right: *Newcastle Quayside.*
Inset: *Baltic Art Centre.*

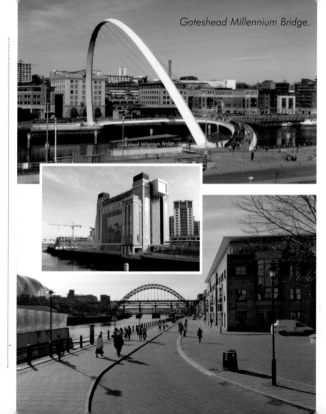

Gateshead Millennium Bridge.

Hall and down the steps to Baltic Square and the Millennium Bridge. Entry to the Sage and Baltic are free.

5 Cross the Millennium Bridge back to the Newcastle side of the river. Turn left (SW) and walk along the quayside for 450 metres, passing the Law Courts and Custom House on your right, to the Tyne Bridge. Continue under the bridge and round to the right, past the circular Guildhall building and over the pedestrian crossing. A few metres to the left is the 5-storey, 16th century, Bessie Surtees' House, now the north-east headquarters of English Heritage. Entry to the house, one of the oldest timber framed houses in Newcastle, is free.

6 From Bessie Surtees' House,

In November 1772, facing opposition from her father, a wealthy banker, Bessie Surtees eloped with, and married John Scott, who later became the first Earl of Eldon and served two terms as Lord Chancellor of England.

return to the pedestrian crossing and follow the road round to the left. This leads beneath a high railway bridge, then up the hill of Dean Street for 200 metres to join Mosley Street.

7 Turn left (SW) and follow Mosley Street, past the Anglican St Nicholas's Cathedral, from which the Central Station can be seen, 400 metres ahead. Return to the station.

Bessie Surtees House.

6 Newburn and Wylam

A beautiful 6-mile walk or cycle ride along the northern and southern banks of the River Tyne.

Wylam holds an important position at the very beginning of the Industrial Revolution, and is the birthplace of George Stephenson and Timothy Hackworth, two of engineering's pioneers. Wylam Waggonway opened in 1748, to carry coal in horse-drawn wagons from Wylam Colliery to keelboats at Lemington, four miles downriver. Between 1813 and 1815, blacksmith, Timothy Hackworth and colliery manager, William Hedley, from Newburn, created Puffing Billy and Wylam Dilly, which remain the oldest surviving steam locomotives in the world. This walk follows the waggonway from Newcastle into Northumberland, then crosses the Tyne to return through Gateshead. It can also be followed, in its entirety by cyclists.

Level: 🐾 🐾
Length: 6 miles
Terrain: Surfaced road, rubble tracks and grassy footpaths.
Park & start: Car park opposite the Sports Centre to the west of Newburn.
Start ref.: NZ 160656
Public transport: Frequent buses to Newburn, from which the start is reached in 800 metres.
Websites: www.gateshead.gov.uk
www.nwt.org.uk

Alpine pennycress.

35

1 Turn right out of the car park and follow the surfaced path (WSW) past the Big Lamp Brewery, and on for 1 kilometre to Blaney Row, terraced houses built in 1889. Carry on either in front of or behind the houses for 200 metres to join the Wylam Waggonway, which is now incorporated into both the Hadrian Cycleway and the Hadrian's Wall Path.

2 Over a distance of 1.5 kilometres, the track converges with the River Tyne, reaching it alongside a sports field, to the north, beyond which the ground rises to Heddon-on-the-Wall.

3 Opposite a signpost indicating George Stephenson's birthplace, go through an opening in the

Blaney Row.

Big Lamp Brewery, Newburn.

George Stephenson was the second of six children, who were brought up in a single room of the Wylam house. The four rooms in the house were each occupied by a different family. At one time, 26 people lived there.

Close House Riverside Nature Reserve is scientifically important because the flowers that grow there, such as alpine pennycress, and spring sandwort are able to tolerate pollution by lead and zinc salts washed there from the mines of the North Pennines.

Grassland, Close House Riverside Nature Reserve.

fence to the riverbank footpath, which after 50 metres, enters the Close House Riverside Nature Reserve. Continue through conifer woodland, which gives way to areas of grassland. Follow any of the parallel footpaths for 700 metres to the next gate. Turn right here to visit George Stephenson's birthplace, now a National Trust property, which stands alongside the waggonway.

4 Either return to the riverbank and follow this for 650 metres, or continue along the waggonway for a similar distance into Wylam. The latter route leads directly to a car park that occupies the site of the former North Wylam railway station.

5 Turn left and cross the bridge over the Tyne to the modern Wylam Station, on the Newcastle - Carlisle line. Turn left again (ENE) and go through the station car park to join the Keelman's Way footpath and cycle track. Follow this for 1100 metres to a golf course.

6 Keep left along the riverbank track for 1600 metres around a curve in the river, to converge again with the railway line. A further 500 metres brings you to a level crossing. Go down past the houses and on for 200 metres to enter Ryton Willows Nature Reserve.

7 Continue along the riverbank for 750 metres to the eastern gate of the reserve, from which point, Newburn Bridge becomes visible and is reached in 500 metres.

George Stephenson's birthplace.

Wylam.

8 Cross the bridge then turn left (NW) past the Boathouse pub, and follow the northern river-bank for 300 metres toward Newburn Leisure Centre. On reaching a wooden footbridge over a stream, take the narrow track (N), which in 150 metres brings you back to the start.

Wylam Station.

The River Tyne is tidal as far upstream as Ryton, 17 miles from the sea. Cleaning up of the once polluted river now means that it is not uncommon to see seals venturing this far from the coast.

An early skirmish in what became the English Civil War took place in 1640 near the present site of Newburn Bridge. A Scottish army of 20 000 invaded in protest at the King's imposition of a new prayer book, and defeated an English army of 3500 soldiers.

River Tyne from Wylam Bridge.

7 Blaydon Burn

A fascinating 3-mile walk on which wildlife and industrial archaeology are encountered in equal measure.

Many of the North-east's once bustling industrial sites have, since their closures, been completely swallowed up by Nature. Others have been so comprehensively landscaped that their past has become almost equally eradicated. Blaydon Burn lies somewhere in the middle. Its steep slopes are heavily wooded, while its more level patches have become wild-flower meadows, and together with its wetland areas, provide thriving habitats for insect and bird life. Yet it is difficult to walk more than a few metres without coming across evidence of the corn mills, brickworks, drift mines and coke and tar works that once dominated the now peaceful valley.

Level: 🍂🍂
Length: 3 miles
Terrain: Rubble tracks and grassy footpaths.
Park & start: About 400 metres along the B6317 from Blaydon to Ryton, a side road leads to Path Head and a car park opposite Summerhill houses.
Start ref.: NZ 177635
Public transport: Buses, Nos 10 and 11 run from Eldon Square, Newcastle and Gateshead Metro Centre stop at Summerhill.
Websites: www.gateshead.gov.uk

Bewes Hills

Path Head

Winlaton

Blaydon Burn

Start of walk.

A695 road above Blaydon
Burn Waggonway.

1 Leave the car park through the gate in the south-west corner. A grassy track leads south to steps, which descend onto the Blaydon Burn Waggonway, just beneath the A695. (Detour for 100-metres to the left to check that the stepping stones across which you will be returning are above water.) Turn right (SW) and follow the waggonway, through a narrow gorge with vegetated, rocky walls, past several small cataracts. After 450 metres, the burn runs through a tunnel beneath the track. A further 250 metres brings you to a more open area, and the site of the former Hobby's Mill.

2 Continue past the millpond on the right, and a little farther, on the left, the remains of Edward Pit and Tar Tunnel. Beyond this, the

Blaydon Burn is one of the region's most important industrial archaeology sites, with more than 100 documented features. During the 18th century, at least eight corn mills were situated here, one of them on the later site of Massey's Forge.

Blaydon Burn Waggonway.

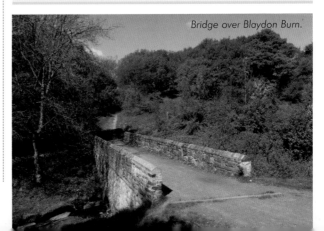

Bridge over Blaydon Burn.

waggonway curves to the south and leads to a stone bridge over the burn.

3 Turn right (NW) across the bridge and go gently uphill for 100 metres, then left over a wooden footbridge and up a set of steps on the right to Herd's House Pond.

4 Follow the footpath along the pond's southern shore. Cross the stile and continue (SSW) along the hedgerow at the side of the field, for 250 metres, past a gate to the next stile. Cross this, turn left (SE) and follow the hedge uphill to the top corner of the field and another stile.

5 Cross this stile, and after 10 metres, turn right and take the track downhill for 300 metres, past the almost overgrown ruins of a former reservoir, to re-join the waggonway on the valley floor.

6 Turn left (NE) and walk past the extensive ruins of the buildings of Bessie Drift Mine. From here, the waggonway runs for 450 metres (NNW) back to the stone bridge (Point 3).

7 100 metres beyond the bridge, turn right (NW) and go steadily uphill for 500 metres and

Sir Joseph Cowen (1800-1873) and his son, Joseph(1829-1900), who owned mines and brickworks in Blaydon Burn, were reforming politicians, who campaigned for workers' rights and voting by secret ballot. They numbered Garibaldi and Karl Marx among their friends.

Herd's House Pond.

Cracks in the ruined walls of the Bessie Pit buildings are now populated by pipistrelle bats.

The Priestman coke ovens produced coal tar, from which petrol, known as Blaydon Benzole, was refined, making this the first place in the world to manufacture petrol from coal.

Ruins of Bessie Drift Mine.
Inset: Edward Pit and Tar Tunnel.

out of the woodland. Continue past a field that was once the site of the Priestman Coke and Tar Works, and on to an electricity sub-station. The houses of Winlaton lie beyond the field.

(8) Go through the kissing gate and gently down past a flower meadow to re-enter the wood. Pass through another kissing gate, down the slope of the gorge and beneath the A695. 30 metres beyond the road, take the steps down to the burn. 20 metres downstream are the remains of the 19th century Massey's Forge. Cross over the stepping stones and turn left (SW). Just before reaching the road, ascend the steps on the right, which lead back to the start.

Massey's Forge.

8 Clockburn Lake

A leisurely 3½-mile walk that includes woodland, lake and riverside meadows, with the possibility of seeing red kites.

The first half of this walk covers part of the Derwent Walk, which follows the line of the Derwent Valley Railway for eleven miles, between Swalwell and Shotley Bridge. Operating from 1867, the railway crossed four viaducts. It carried iron ore to Consett Steel Works, coal and bricks to Newcastle and more than half-a-million passengers each year, until its closure in 1962. During the 18th and 19th centuries, Crowley's Ironworks, then the largest in Europe, occupied the present site of Derwenthaugh Country Park. In 1928, the land was taken over by the Derwenthaugh Coke Works, which continued to operate until 1986. The route can be followed by cyclists and horse riders.

Level: 🥾
Length: 3½ miles
Terrain: Surfaced road and rubble tracks.
Park & start: Swalwell Visitor Centre, behind Blaydon Rugby Club.
Start ref.: NZ 197620
Public transport: Nos 45 and 46 buses from Newcastle to Blaydon Rugby Club and Swalwell via Gateshead Metro Centre.
Websites: www.gateshead.gov.uk
www.northernkites.org.uk

Cowslip.

Map labels:
Blaydon
Winlaton
Axwell Park
Hagg Hill
Winlaton Mill
ntley Wood
Whickham
Derwenthaugh Country Park

1 Take the track opposite the door of the visitor centre, which leads (SSE) for 150 metres through trees and around the edge of a meadow to join the Derwent Walk track. Turn right (SW) as indicated toward Rowlands Gill. This former railway track leads past old station walls and a ruined bridge, and across a steep, wooded hillside, with occasional glimpses to the right, down to the River Derwent.

2 After 2.5 kilometres, the track reaches the entrance to Derwenthaugh Country Park. Carry on past this for 100 metres to the centre of the Nine Arches viaduct, from which there are superb views over the river. The wooded slopes to the south belong to the National Trust's Gibside Estate, above which rises a monument to Liberty. This is also the place from which you are most likely to see red kites and buzzards circling above the valley. The best view of the viaduct itself can be obtained by descending steps to Lockhaugh Meadows from the western end of the bridge.

3 Return over the viaduct and

Swalwell: Sign to start of Derwent Walk.

Gibside Estate from Nine Arches viaduct.

Nine Arches viaduct from Lockhaugh Meadows.

The 150-metre-long, 24-metre-high Lockhaugh, or Nine Arches viaduct was built in 1836, because the 11th Earl of Strathmore refused to allow the railway to cross Gibside Estate. It was widened to carry a double track between 1905 and 1908.

enter the country park. Take the surfaced road to the left (NNW), which circles the base of a hill. The hill can be easily ascended, as a detour, to view the viaduct and the ruins of the 13th century Hollinside Manor, to the south-east. Re-join the roadway, which follows a loop in the river, for 800 metres, to a stone bridge, built in 1998. Cross the bridge to reach the slope that leads down to Clockburn Lake.

Following their re-introduction between 2004 and 2006, after an absence of 170 years, red kites have successfully bred in the Derwent Valley, and are now spreading farther afield, to the edge of the Pennines and into Teesdale.

Cycleway marker at the entrance to the Derwenthaugh Country Park.

In 1767, John Lyon, 9th Earl of Strathmore, married Mary Eleanor Bowes, owner of Gibside Estate. They became ancestors of the British Royal Family through Elizabeth Bowes-Lyon, the Queen Mother, who often visited Gibside as a child.

4 Follow either route around the lake. That to the south is slightly longer, but more picturesque, and gives easier access to the shore, from which swans, coot, moorhens, mallards and tufted ducks may be

Sculpture at the entrance to the Derwenthaugh Country Park

River Derwent from 1998 stone bridge.

seen. The paths join beyond the north-east shore.

5 Continue for 500 metres, past patches of woodland and wildflower meadows that support numerous butterflies, to the Winlaton Mill car park, and for another 400 metres to the Spa Well car park.

6 The footpath follows the river bank, past Blaydon Tennis Club and alongside a weir, to meet the Blaydon-Rowlands Gill road at a bridge.

7 Turn right over the bridge and continue for a further 400 metres to return to the Swalwell Visitor Centre.

The Column of Liberty, on the Gibside Estate, stands taller than London's Nelson's Column, and pre-dates its New York namesake by a century.

Outflow of Clockburn Lake into River Derwent.

9 Watergate Forest Park

A most enjoyable 3¼-mile walk that combines semi-natural woodland with newly landscaped country park.

For more than 30 years, following its closure, the Watergate Colliery left a legacy of utter dereliction, from which visitors were excluded. The land was bought from the National Coal Board by Gateshead Council in the late 1980s, and with the aid of various grants, transformed beyond recognition. Opened to the public in 2000, Watergate Forest Park still has a somewhat manicured appearance, yet is as attractive as other sites of similar

origin, where Nature has been given a free reign. The network of footpaths, cycle tracks and bridleways, decorated by imaginative sculptures, allow many variations that can be explored at will.

Level: 🥾 🥾
Length: 3¼ miles.
Terrain: Rubble tracks and grassy footpaths.
Park & start: Turn west off A1 at Team Valley - Lobley Hill roundabout. At next roundabout, turn right onto Whickham Highway. After 250 metres, turn left into car park.
Start ref.: NZ 229606
Public transport: Frequent buses to Lobley Hill and Whickham Highway.
Websites: www.gateshead.gov.uk

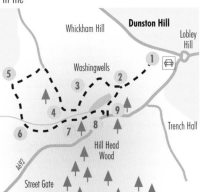

Tufted duck.

Mining sculpture.

 1 Leave the car park through the gateway in the south-west corner, and follow the broad bridleway/cycle track for 200 metres, past three metal sculptures, to a junction of tracks. Take the path to the right, which drops gently downhill for a further 200 metres to the north-eastern end of the lake, and a small dipping pond.

2 Keep right (WNW) and follow the pathway through a hazel

Flames to Flowers sculpture at entrance to Watergate Forest Park.

plantation. This swings round to the left above a boulder slope, with good views across the lake. Turn sharp right at the next junction, and continue to the top of the hill, which is crowned by a large steel sculpture: Green Heart.

3 At the next junction of tracks, again keep right and follow

Dipping pond.

Boulder slope and lake.
Inset: *Green Heart sculpture.*

The wildflower meadow, south of Washingwells Farm is the site of a Roman fort, discovered by aerial survey.

the path that swings west, then south to another junction. Turn right again, and after 50 metres, reach a gateway leading into a strip of woodland.

4 Take the footpath (NNW) that leads uphill to the side of a wildflower meadow. Continue through an opening in the hedge into the next field, and cross this (could be muddy at times) to Washingwells Farm. Follow the fence round left to join a track that runs WSW for 300 metres, crossing the northern end of the woodland strip, to the corner of the field beyond.

Bridge between the lake and Washingwell Wood.

During the 1990s, a fire in the colliery spoil heaps burned for several months, and was eventually extinguished by covering it with clay.

5 Turn left (SSE) and go gently downhill for 300 metres to enter the next strip of mature conifers, known as Washingwell Wood.

6 Cross the footbridge and turn left (ESE). The track follows the gorge above the southern bank of the stream. After 200 gently rising

The footpath through the south of the reserve follows the line of a branch of the Tanfield Railway, which from 1840, transported coal from Watergate Colliery to the River Tyne at Dunston.

The Lake.

metres, it reaches a patch of open ground, next to the A692 road. This is the former site of Fugar Manor House. Go down the steps leading east and curving to north-east, to the bottom of the gorge.

7 Cross the metal footbridge and turn right (E) along the northern bank for 100 metres to the next bridge. Cross this, and after a short distance, drop down and over the third bridge. 100 metres beyond this, take

Washingwell Wood, also known locally as Bluebell Wood, because of its spring flora, is an ancient, semi-natural woodland. Its conifers were used as roofing props in the Watergate colliery.

the fourth, and much larger bridge across the south-west end of the lake.

8 Turn left (E) and continue to yet another bridge. Rather than cross this, take the detour to the right, which in 100 metres, circles a waterfall and the Floating Rocks

sculpture, before returning to the lakeside path.

9 The path now follows the lake shore (NE) for 200 metres, and continues in the same direction for a further 400 metres to the car park.

Floating Rocks sculpture and waterfall.

10 **Causey Arch**

A continuously interesting 4-mile walk through fields and a wooded gorge, past the world's first railway bridge.

The main Tanfield line was built in 1647 to transport coal from the local collieries to ships waiting on the banks of the Tyne. The rails and wagons were wooden and traction was provided by horses. The line was in continuous use, carrying both freight and passengers, until 1964. Of the 2½ miles of track that remain, the section between Sunniside and Causey Arch was built in 1725, making it the oldest surviving working railway in the world. The line was taken over in the 1970s by a group of enthusiastic volunteers, the Tanfield Railway Association, who repair, maintain and operate the railway throughout the year.

Level: ♥ ♥
Length: 4 miles
Terrain: Surfaced road, rubble tracks and grassy footpaths.
Park & start: Car park at Andrews House Station on the Tanfield Railway, on the A6076 Sunniside - Stanley road.
Start ref.: NZ 209573
Public transport: Buses from Newcastle, Eldon Square and Gateshead Metro station (not Sunday).
Websites: www.tanfieldrailway.co.uk

Andrews House Station.

Maintenance is carried out in the Marley Hill Engine Shed,
next to Andrews House Station. Having operated since
1854, this is thought to be the world's second oldest
railway shed. Visitors are welcome.

Cross the railway bridge and continue (SW) along the track passing debris of the Marley Hill Engine Sheds, which lie to the right. The track leads downhill for 500 metres, then turns left (S) and carries on for 250 metres to a gate beside some ruined buildings.

2 Turn left and follow the fence to the corner, then cross the

stile into the field on the right. The path now runs downhill for 400 metres, then over a footbridge and

Locomotives in Marley Hill engine shed.

Marley Hill engine shed.

through a gate onto a road at the entrance to a wooded gorge.

3 Turn right along the road for 50 metres, then left onto the woodland path, signposted to Causey Arch. The track meanders across two concrete bridges to the first quarried face. Across to the left is a culvert, built to carry the stream through the railway embankment, when it was built in 1765. Cross the first of four wooden bridges over the burn. The

Built in 1725-6, at a cost of £12 000, Causey Arch was, for thirty years, the longest single-span bridge in England, reaching 32 metres across the gorge, at a height of 24 metres above the river.

Climber abseiling down Causey Quarry.

Above: *Causey Arch.*
Below: *Causey Arch station and siding.*

second bridge stands beneath the quarry crag, which is now an important rock climbing venue. Continue up the gorge. As you reach the fourth bridge, Causey Arch comes into view. Carry on to the base of this.

(4) Climb the steps to the right, to the west end of the arch. Follow the track to the right, (SW), to a fork. Take the right fork, up to and over a stile into a field. The path runs for 600 metres following the field edge, through two gates and along a farm track. Where this turns sharply

Causey Arch never felt the weight of iron rails or a steam train, but fell into disuse after a fire destroyed the Tanfield colliery in 1739.

left, toward sewage works, climb over the stile on the right and go along the edge of the next field. A few metres after passing through the next fence, cross the stile on the left and go down the side of the field for 250 metres (SSE) to a road running between a farm and the sewage works, at the eastern end of a wood.

5 A muddy track to the left, runs uphill, through the wood, to a clearing. Keep to the right side of the clearing, and after 100 metres, follow another path through the trees, which leads down to an iron girder bridge at the East Tanfield end of the gorge. Turn left (NE) and after

80 metres, cross the bridge over the burn. The track converges with the railway, and crosses the line, to continue on the other side. It leads past the site of a haulage engine, which once pulled wagons from East Tanfield. The track eventually descends across the railway line again at Causey Arch station.

6 A surfaced path runs for 200 metres, after which a set of steps leads down into the gorge. These are followed by a gentle ascent to the Causey Arch car park.

7 Leave the car park by its main exit. Cross the road to the hotel. Turn left (NE) and walk along the pavement for 900 metres to the Andrews House car park.

Replica coal wagon.

View of the gorge from Causey Arch.